Poetry Pod:
Water with a Twist of Sublime

Christina M. Eder

Felicity Press

Christina M. Eder

Copyright © 2022 by CHRISTINA M. Eder

Cover by Red Paint Spilman, assisted by Chris Woods
Edited by Wesley D. Sims
Layout by Rita M. Reali

No portion of this book may be reproduced in any form or by any means, including electronic storage and retrieval systems, without the expressed prior written permission of the author.

Connect with Christina on Facebook (www.facebook.com/EDERAuthor).

P.O. Box 5181
Oak Ridge, TN 37830

www.gueststarcoaching.com

Eder, Christina M.
POETRY POD: Water with a Twist of Sublime

ISBNs:
(paperback) 978-1-7346596-6-5
(ebook)   978-1-7346596-7-2

Printed in the U.S.A.
First American edition, February 2022

Other Books by Christina M. Eder:

Life's Too Short for Dull Razors, Cheap Pens, and Worn Out Underwear

The FROG Blog: Learning on a Lily Pad

UNTHAWED: Lessons from a Frozen Lily Pad

KNEE DEEP: A 9-Month Whirlpool of Handwritten Letters to the Creator

TADPOLES: Tiny Tales from Freshwater Adventures

Author Invitation

I love getting feedback from readers. Your input adds to my writing development. Please consider posting an online review, sharing my books, viewing my website or even writing me a note. (I most appreciate snail mail.)

Christina M. Eder
PO Box 5181
Oak Ridge, TN 37830

www.gueststarcoaching.com

"...and every gifted artisan in whose heart the Lord had put wisdom, everyone whose heart was stirred, to come and do the work."

— ***Exodus 36:1***

Acknowledgments

I find that writing acknowledgments is one of my strongest challenges in a book's process. I worry I'll omit someone's name. I wonder whether everyone knows how they've added value to my life. Each person, in various ways, has breathed life into my literary development.

Often, a writer's life can seem like a game. Every player in my game has helped me win somehow. Therefore, I will intentionally exclude all names in this acknowledgement. Whoever reads this, thank you! Please accept my simulated bear hug of gratitude. You all have affected my life's adventure ☺

Back Story of *Poetry Pod*

If someone had told me my series of *FROG Blog* books would include a poetry collection, I'd have responded with (tongue-in-cheek) "unedited free verse." My prior poetry exposure had been limited to nursery rhymes, limericks or whatever I was required to read in school. I hadn't practiced poetry much beyond "Mary had a Little Lamb" or "Baa, Baa, Black Sheep."

I met someone at a writers' conference who said she dabbled in poetry as her break from technical writing. To hone her craft, she attends poetry readings and enters contests. Her persistent submissions have gone either unpublished or unrecognized. She said much prose becomes a literary homeless community: "It's like writers give birth to poetic word babies and contest judges deem them orphans. In a sense, poets have created a homeless community. We have creations that have been overlooked and abandoned; ideas that have been misunderstood or stolen."

This conference participant encouraged me to talk with other poets. I wanted to hear what intrigued them about this magical-to-me writing style. After countless conversations and months of interviews, I discovered a consistent theme: People find clarity and solace through their poetry and free-verse pieces.

I primarily write creative nonfiction pieces, but – after hearing some incredible verses – I wanted to give poets a voice for their backstories and poems. After months of redirecting my projects, I shifted gears and began poet interviews.

During these interviews, poets shared the raw, sometimes traumatic situations that caused them to flex their tenacity muscle. Many of them penned their vicious experiences by writing under a cryptic frame to shelter themselves from self-implosion. Free-verse writing provided spiritual refreshment when they felt threatened by abuse and neglect.

I learned how people crafted poetry to find hope and courage to persevere. Their pens and paper generated written beacons of light. A few poets said that sometimes they grabbed whatever writing utensil or paper scrap they could find to cathartically direct their pain to pen (side note: I got to enjoy animated stories about what people use for pen-and-paper substitutes... napkins, toilet paper, grocery receipts and their arms. Jumbo green crayons, eyeliner and construction pencils also served as emergency writing utensils, according to some interviewees).

Some people trusted me to listen to their writing from deep wells in their heart. After multiple conversations and unexpected connections, I felt compelled to find a home for these poets to house their craft.

Some well-seasoned poets joined me in shaping this *Poetry Pod*. They have taught, critiqued and fostered my poetic development. Professional poets linked their proficiency with my inexperience and I'm grateful for their generosity. They connected our once-homeless stories to a larger community.

I expanded the scope of my literary-anthology collections to include *Poetry Pod: Water with a Twist of Sublime*. What follows is 37 of my best-of-what-I-know-now poems and 30 treasures from 15 fellow *Poetry Pod* teammates.

Poetry in motion from the lily pad of life,

Christina

Dedications

I dedicate *Poetry Pod: Water with a Twist of Sublime* to Mom, Chris and Wendy Woods and Rita M. Reali.

Dedicated to my mom, Carol Lynn. She taught me to fall in love with words. She read my first story I wrote as her birthday gift when I was six years old. My amateur publishing house produced crookedly stapled pages and stick-figure illustrations. Mom continued to read my numerous publications: school papers, newsletters, magazine articles and newspaper columns, until she moved to heaven in 2015. I miss her edits, feedback and countless Scrabble games. Mom, until we write again!

A special dedication to my literary birth dad, Chris Woods. He published my first book, *Life's Too Short for Dull Razors, Cheap Pens, and Worn-Out Underwear.* Chris encouraged me to turn my online FROG Blog essays into a book collection. That led to a five-book series, beginning with *FROG Blog: Learning on a Lily Pad.* Chris took a risk on my new-to-the-book-publishing venture and I'm intensely grateful for Chris and his wife Wendy. They've guided and cheered me on during all phases of each book.

Rita M. Reali fulfills this book's dedication. Rita has an extensive resume of professional experience and awards in highly respected arenas. Her actions follow from a heart of integrity. She invites mutually benefitting relationships with her respect, kindness and attentiveness. She shares contagious frivolity and becomes most animated when she's telling a story. Rita has added a standard of excellence to my life story.

Contents

Author Invitation iv
Acknowledgments vi
Backstory of *Poetry Pod* vii
Dedications x

Section One 2
Literary Birth Mom 4
There's a Time for Everything, But Not
Everything All at Once 6
What Am I Waiting For? 8
Self-Starter 9
Tender Bidding 10
Every Day is Judgment Day 11
Cross, His Destiny 12
Marching Orders 13
A Wonder Full Life 13

Haiku
The Land Before Eternity 14
Bi-focals 14
Collision Course 14
Pinstripes 14
A Field of Dreams 15
Generous Conduit 15
Branching Out 15
Bi-lingual 15
Expelled 16
Downfall 16

Section Two 18
Hands (author unknown) 19
Turning (Jere Andrews) 21
Beyond (Jere Andrews) 23
Death and Taxes (Mallorie Clark) 25
Breathe (Mallorie Clark) 26
Look for the Light (Candice Eder) 27
Happiness (Candice Eder) 28
A Chronology (Maribeth Hunt) 29
Missy in the Snow (Maribeth Hunt) 31
Bereft (Maribeth Hunt) 32
One Red Rose (Jean Jordan) 34
My Last Words (Jean Jordan) 36
My Son (Jennifer Korell) 38
I'm Praying for You (Jennifer Korell) 40
Watching My Christy Grow (Carol Lynn Mahr) 42
Why I Like My Family (Carol Lynn Mahr) ... 45
Coming Home (Carol Lynn Mahr) 47
That New Girl (Ericka Mitchell-Diaz) 50
Twilight Ballet (Rita M. Reali) 52
Family Trees (Rita M. Reali, writing as Gary J. Sheldon) 54
Resurrection (Wesley D. Sims) 57
Perspective (Wesley D. Sims) 59
One Unknown (Wesley D. Sims) 61
Jonathan Livingston Seagull Bakes Sourdough (David Stratton) 65
She's Gone (David Stratton) 69
Life at Bird Feeder (Sandra Kay Stratton) .. 74
Omnipotent (Larry Vittone) 76
Invisible (Larry Vittone) 78
Whispers in the Night (Susan Vittone) 80
Where is God (Susan Vittone) 81

Section Three 84
Endless Counting 85
Please RSVP 86
Speak Up 87
Dinner Time 88
Deployed 89
Peace in Pieces 90
Perpetual Poverty 91
Universal Obesity 93

Haiku
Haiku Verse 95
Last Respects 95
A Moon's Lullaby 95
Summer Delight 96
Some More Summer Delight 96
Circle of Life 96
Surrender 97
One Smile at a Time 97
Cake Walk 97
Lucky Verde 97

POETRY POD: Water with a Twist of Sublime

Christina M. Eder

Poetry Pod:
Water with a Twist of Sublime

Christina M. Eder

POETRY POD: Water with a Twist of Sublime

Section One

Pain & Wonder

I stand before you tonight to represent the people who do not count: The poor, the poets, and monks. As long as there are people who are trying to realize the divine in themselves, there shall be hope in the world. We do not exist for ourselves.
— **Thomas Merton**

Christina M. Eder

POETRY POD: Water with a Twist of Sublime

Literary Birth Mom

She was created to birth literary essence
Her mind, a fertile womb
conceiving inspiration, curious bliss
She senses a whim awakening
as contemplation leaps
Limited confinement.
Musings refuse suffocation
Reflection must shine
Nature takes its written course
She begins courting publishers
Query after query, date after date,
the birth Mom attracts a suitable match
to raise her upcoming child
and move to a Publishing House
Together they learn to communicate
until they settle upon a date
to start their family of books
As the delivery date draws near,
author and publisher prepare
to birth a literary genius
who could become
the world's best seller

These parents host baby showers.
They send birth announcements
to proclaim their upcoming bundle of joy.
Laboring contractions
Shifting tension
Past tense, future tense
present tense proclaims birth
After intense labor, Baby Book is delivered,
Newborn cries
Utters gurgled gibberish

Christina M. Eder

The Mom sits in wonder
as she celebrates her newborn's
entry into the world
She speaks life over it
as she anticipates her readers
will love her book
as she treasures it.
Sentences evolve into awkward paragraphs
until the polish of puberty
completes its edit cycle
Tired. Content.
Her pain is worth the net return.
A smile crosses her face
as she gives a thumbs up
to a five-star sky,
knowing she'll conceive again.
One birth is only the beginning
of a series of literary babies.
She was born to birth books.

POETRY POD: Water with a Twist of Sublime

"A Time for Everything, But Not Everything at Once"
(An Author's Living Translation)
— *(Birthed from Eccl. 3: 1-8)*

To everything there is a season,
A time for every purpose under heaven:

A time for "In the Beginning,"
A time for "The End;"

A time to query,
A time to publish;

A time to let a storyline die,
A time to resurrect a plotline;

A time for drafting,
A time for editing;

A time to celebrate a contact,
A time to handle a rejection letter;

A time to read tragedy,
A time to read comedy;

A time to buy books,
A time to sell books;

A time for writer's flow,
A time for writer's block;

A time for researching,
A time for writing;

Christina M. Eder

A time for creative writing,
A time for technical writing;

A time to read others' writing,
A time to have my writing read;

A time to interview,
A time to be interviewed;

A time for novels,
A time for nonfiction;

A time for writer's conferences,
A time for writer's retreats.

A time for everything
A time for nothing.

POETRY POD: Water with a Twist of Sublime

What Am I Waiting For?

The day to begin
The day to end
School to start
School to finish
A grocery line
A food-pantry line

>A date
>A break-up
>A marriage
>A divorce
>A question
>An answer
>A friend to come
>An enemy to leave

A birth
A death
Summer
Winter
A respite
A healing

>Waiting to inhale
>Waiting to exhale
>One breath at a time
>Will it be worth the wait?

Christina M. Eder

Self-Starter

Self employed
Self-imploding
A dream
A nightmare
Depending on
The state of self

POETRY POD: Water with a Twist of Sublime

Tender Bidding

Flow or Fixate
Weightless or Burdensome
Invite or Demand
Offer or Sacrifice
Remember or Don't Forget
Unexpected or Routine
Divine or Coincidence
Reflect or Scrutinize
Different or Wrong
Wished or Expected
Blooms or Thorns
Butterfly or Hornet
Both take flight
Which will land gently?

Christina M. Eder

Every Day is Judgment Day

    Judging
        Being Judged
    Microscopic lens
        Telescopic vision
    Labeling
        Being Labeled
    Living under a label
    Being judged only by our Creator

POETRY POD: Water with a Twist of Sublime

Cross, His Destiny

No phone
Pre-video
Pre-internet
Delivered to teenage mother
Last name unknown
Eternally remembered as
A One-name Wonder
Misunder-
stood
Homeless
Penniless
Priceless
Saved
Healed
Celebrated
Rejoiced
Shunned
Mocked
Crucified
centuries
ago

Christina M. Eder

Marching Orders

Living a standard of excellence
Without a sense of permanence
On this earthly mission field
Temporarily deployed
For 50   70   Perhaps 100 years.
I serve on this planet's task force
Under a General Commander's orders
One day I will return
To my Permanent Post
To live a higher standard of excellence
In my Eternal Home.
A wounded warrior
Waiting for complete healing
Becoming what I believe

A Wonder Full Life

If curiosity is said to kill the cat
Have we become a world of scaredy cats?
If we cease to be curious
Will our creative life die?

POETRY POD: Water with a Twist of Sublime

HAIKU

The Land Before Eternity

Fiercely the clock ticks.
Redeem unexpended hours.
Part earth. Part heaven.

Bi-focals

Seeing God through pained
Glass windows, raining color
One tear at a time.

Collision Course

Knowing right from wrong,
Rebellious forces battle.
Opposition strikes.

Pinstripes

Bright candy striper.
Volunteer cheerleader smiles,
Dispensing sunshine.

Christina M. Eder

A Field of Dreams

Written flowers pen
Blooming possibilities.
Lush fragrant treasure.

Generous Conduit

Demolished walls. Gate.
Fence. Bridge. Viaduct. Passage.
Devoid brick. Kindness.

Branching Out

Palm Sunday. Holding
Universe in His hand. Now.
Forever. Amen.

Bi-lingual

One speaks parables.
One speaks science. Both seek to
Explore connections.

POETRY POD: Water with a Twist of Sublime

Expelled

Social outcast begs
Bread. Hope baits courage. Cast out.
Empty net. Starved.

Downfall

He's eating poison
Salivates, Divides, Devours
Man's venomous pride

Christina M. Eder

Section 2

Poetry Pod Teammates

Every heart sings a song, incomplete, until another heart whispers back. Those who wish to sing always find a song. At the touch of a lover, everyone becomes a poet.
— **Plato**

Christina M. Eder

Submitted from unknown author in *Wisconsin* magazine July 1975 (Page 3).

"I would like to close with the words my daughter Caryl wrote for me..."

Hands

    Paralyzed Hands
    Helping Hands
    Tired Hands
    Old Hands
    Young Hands
    Strong Hands
    Weak Hands
    Praying Hands
    Destructive Hands
    Rough Hands
        Soft Hands
        Lord, which are mine?
Hands that work
Hands that embrace
Hands that touch
Hands with feeling
Hands that are cold

Hands that are warm
Hands that reach out
Hands which hold
Hands that comfort
    Hands for you
    Lord, which are mine?
Meaningless Hands
Hating Hands
Loving Hands
Caring Hands
Nervous Hands
    Hurting Hands
    Lord, which are mine?
Burden Carrying Hands
Serving Hands
    Non-caring Hands
    Lord, could these be mine?
Taking Hands
Giving Hands
    Tell me Lord.
Where do my Hands fit?

Christina M. Eder

Turning

Jere Andrews

With life's blessings to be blessed,
and all is at rest and calm,
when earthly things are plentiful,
many forget where the blessings come from.

A little affliction, tribulation, or persecution,
could be a blessing in disguise.
It may serve for a new awakening,
with events that can open the eyes.

When blinded by the things of life,
often the important is laid aside.
It may well require a dose of strife
for one to ever realize.

Too many days are wasted,
in them are found no rest.
Turn to seek first the kingdom of God,
and all of his righteousness.

To turn now to accept,
and to lean on the one who can.
To escape the hold of self's grip,
that is all too common to man.

POETRY POD: Water with a Twist of Sublime

To turn now to surrender,
forsaking the often struggle with self.
To cease from being a pretender,
now to seek God and no one else.

To turn and allow Him in,
with free reign then to rule.
To lead you away from all sin,
and to give Him the worship he is due.

To turn and allow self,
the avenue to make it so.
To live for God as one should,
as toward the end of life all go.

Turning was developed from an earlier writing when I was thinking about the recent events in our world. I am faced with the reality of how fragile life is and how many blessings are often taken for granted. Seeing that everything physical can be threatened, or even taken away. Ultimately, I understand the spiritual is eternal and available if we will turn to God.

Christina M. Eder

Beyond

Jere Andrews

Beyond the present's senseless turmoil,
beyond that which will soon be gone.
Not understanding it is only temporary,
and unable to see what is beyond.

Beyond those bounds of human sight,
on past the realm of physical thought.
From earthly blinders we will be freed,
then to see all truth, as we ought.

Beyond the present's restraint of time,
its coming is sure on someday's tomorrow.
When times days will no longer bind,
there is a place of no more sorrow.

Beyond the mental grasp of many,
of closed minds which will not allow.
Refusing to consider the possibility,
that it is all true, some way, some how.

Beyond all but for a faithful few,
who in their lives will overcome.
Those willing to walk the straight and narrow,
until God comes to take them home.

POETRY POD: Water with a Twist of Sublime

Beyond was written about what comes after this life. From my view, this present world, with its sorrow and turmoil is only temporary. Events in life, good or bad, will pass away. What's important awaits after our time on earth.

Jere Andrews is a "mostly" retired farmer from middle Tennessee. He enjoys his family which includes Wanda, his wife of 41 years, two sons and daughters-in-law. Jere and Wanda have nine grandchildren – four boys and five girls. He began writing in memory of his and Wanda's daughter Courtney, his mother and brother. Their daughter passed away at 33 years old and his mother and brother died from pulmonary fibrosis. All three deaths happened within a span of two years. Jere says writing, for him, is mind healing.

Death and Taxes

Mallorie Clark

Sometimes all in life that's promised is death and taxes.
Sometimes the world seems to have fallen off of its axis.

We have the choice to create our days.
Even in the bad moments, everything is a phase.

Just hold on. It won't be long.
There are ten beautiful things for every wrong.

Hold your head high.
Look up to the sky.

You're never alone.
Even when all you can do is grumble and groan.

It's always the darkest before the dawn.
Always believe that hope is never gone.

For we were made for more than death and taxes.
When you believe this, you will realign your earth's axis.

POETRY POD: Water with a Twist of Sublime

Breathe

Mallorie Clark

When the breath in your lungs feels stale, just breathe.
When the blood in your veins feels thick, just breathe.
When the world feels way too loud, just breathe.
From oxygen to carbon dioxide, as goes stress to peace.
When things get too much, just breathe.

Breathe and *Death* and *Taxes* derived from lessons and blessin's from what was administered this past year in my life.

I'm **Mallorie Clark**, a mother of two beautiful little girls, a high-energy Rotterman and a shy guinea pig. I've made meditation and therapy a huge part of my life – not just for myself, but also the lives I'm responsible for. I've thought that a bad moment determines a bad life. I'm learning it's extremely hard to grasp when my human brain forgets how supernaturally awesome and wonderfully we are made! Everybody is capable and deserves to find inner peace, even in unconventional times. I had to have a heartbreaking experience to help me see my misguided thought pattern. I hope my poetry pieces help knock some dust off the hearts of others, too!

Look For the Light

Candice Eder

A weary head, a hopeless heart
A dream of life left in the dark
The tears – they fall and soak my skin
I'm ready for life to start again
I close my eyes and begin to pray
Lord, the world can't continue this way
I ask for healing, I ask for guidance
I sit alone in a room full of silence
This new monster has come to stay
But things won't always be in dismay
I put my faith and trust in you
I know your salvation will bring us through
I politely ask God for simple things
Over my body, peace this brings
He says, "Do not worry through the night
I'm always here, look for the light"

Look for the Light is a culmination of feelings from the previous year. I believe God will never forsake us, even during our most trying times. No matter what, it is always important to see the bright side of things.

Happiness

Candice Eder

What is happiness? you ask.
It's breakfast for dinner.
It's saying, "I love you," in more ways than one.
It's sleeping in on a Sunday.
It's looking into your daughter's eyes for the first time.
It's achieving a goal you thought you couldn't.
It's taking the first sip of coffee in the morning.
It's helping your neighbor.
It's a steaming hot shower after a long day.
It's your favorite song on repeat.
It's helping those in need.
It's smiling at a stranger to brighten their day.
What is happiness? you ask.
Happiness is whatever you make it.

Happiness came to me after asking myself, "What really makes you happy?" After reflecting and coming up with more than one answer, I realized happiness is whatever you need it to be in that exact moment. Be your own happiness!

Candice Eder—I'm a wife. I am a mother of two beautiful girls, who own my entire heart. I am a nursing student. Hiking the Kentucky mountains brings me the greatest joy.

Christina M. Eder

A Chronology

Maribeth Hunt

Pain
Back surgery
Pandemic
Masks
Isolation
Death
Governor Cuomo documenting
Government denying
No sports
No employment
Stores closing
Comorbidities
Netflix bingeing
Racial reckoning
I hope
Cat appearing out of nowhere
Wants to be inside, but
He doesn't feel well
Sick, Mean
Finally recovering
Sports in bubbles
A new norm?
Vaccines
A new hope?

This poem starts in January 2020 when I had excruciating back pain. I could barely move. *A Chronology* shuttles my experiences during a year when I tried encompassing what was happening in the country/world. In the middle of the year, a cat showed up in my house. I didn't know he was sick; he looked and acted healthy. He bit and I thought he was mean, but I was wrong. Together, we figured it out.

Looking back, 2020 was one of the most devastating and divisive years I have experienced in my 71 years.

Christina M. Eder

Missy in the Snow

Maribeth Hunt

Cat bounds through fresh snow
Deeper than she is tall, harsh
Searching for shelter

Missy in the Snow came to me from a time I worked overseas in Vienna and the surrounds. When I lived in Vienna proper, I had no pets. I moved to Klosterneuburg on the Cloister Mountain, which is like a suburb. I needed company and missed having cats, so I adopted two. They were litter mates and the runts of the litter. The house was in the hills, overlooking the Danube River, and when winter came, we would often get over a foot of snow. Missy never weighed over 6½ pounds, so she was really small.

I like the structure of haiku to paint a picture in few words. This haiku is a picture of my cat Missy going out onto the patio to greet almost two feet of snow. She found a clear space under a discarded Christmas tree.

POETRY POD: Water with a Twist of Sublime

Bereft

Maribeth Hunt

Illness consuming,
Death, destruction, riots, split, reft
America struggles

Bereft is my haiku about the last couple of years and how the political climate has changed within the United States. We should not be struggling. We are a world power. I was raised in a politically active household and have a degree in political science. I consider myself an extremely "political person" and this colors my writings. This political bend has been reinforced by working overseas for 20 years. Although my poems may not relate to you as they do to me, I hope they paint a picture. Your picture will not be the same picture I had when I wrote it. It's your picture. Make it yours.

Maribeth Hunt was born in Nebraska and grew up in Colorado. She defines herself as a perpetual wanderer, moving from Colorado to Washington State, California, Vienna, Austria, and, finally, Knoxville, Tennessee. Maribeth holds degrees in political science and chemistry and has spent her professional life in nuclear sciences. She was in space nuclear power, an International Safeguards Inspector,

Christina M. Eder

and Safeguards Training Officer with the United Nations International Atomic Energy Agency in Vienna. In 2005, The Agency and its employees were awarded the Nobel Peace Prize. Maribeth retired and lives in Knoxville, Tennessee, where she focuses on her cats and writing.

POETRY POD: Water with a Twist of Sublime

One Red Rose

Jean Jordan

After coming home from work one day
Never once did I ever think
That I would see ONE RED ROSE
In a vase next to my sink
My husband has done so much for me
More than I can ever tell
But the minute I saw that ONE RED ROSE
Put me back under his spell
Him being a tall, strong man
No one would ever guess
Just how safe that rose would be
As he held it in his gentle hands
ONE RED ROSE may not mean much to you
But in my head in a whirl
The thought behind him getting that rose
Got my heart, when I was just a girl
There've been many gifts from him
The forty-two years since we've wed
But none have ever meant as much to me
As my single ONE ROSE so RED
Now one of my special places
In my mind when I often think
How special that single ONE RED ROSE
Was to me, in a vase sitting next to my sink!

Special note from Christina: In 2018, my neighbor and author friend, **Jean Jordan** encouraged me to create a *Poetry Pod* in my *FROG Blog* series. I had little experience with poetry, but she said she'd partner with me to bring this project to life.

On March 12, 2020, at 83 years old, Miss Jean moved to heaven and our *Poetry Pod* sat dormant. She planned to share "One Red Rose" and "My Last Words" from her published book, *Jean's Thoughts in Rhyme*. Miss Jean captures her life message as only this friend, mentor and fellow soldier on earth could.

Readers, if you get to heaven before I do, please hug Miss Jean for me. Tell her I'll join her "when God has finished purifying me." I'm learning to trust that purification process like her life quest taught me.

POETRY POD: Water with a Twist of Sublime

My Last Words

Jean Jordan

This poem was read at Miss Jean's funeral on March 15, 2020.

When you're standing here tonight
Please don't shed any tears
Just because I've left without you
Doesn't mean that I don't care
I must make this trip by myself
But I'm not making it all alone
While on earth Jesus walked with me
Now He's taking me to my new home
I'll be walking the Streets of Heaven
The Bible tells me they're paved with gold
And I'll have a brand new body
I'll never be sick and I'll never grow old
All these years I've lived for Jesus
To be with Him has been my goal
On this earth I've shared my life with you
Long ago I gave Jesus my Soul
I hope the time I've been around you
That you have seen my little light shine
It's been my pleasure of talking to you
My words to you I prayed were kind
No more walking through the valleys
No more torment of being afraid
Walking through those gates of Glory

Christina M. Eder

> Rejoicing forever because I'm saved
> Now you're paying me your last visit
> And I ask you to please not cry
> Come to see me in my mansion
> When you come to the other side!

From the back jacket of *Jean's Thoughts, in Rhyme*:

This sampling illustrates Jean Jordan's unique and upbeat outlook on life as reflected in her poetry throughout her life. Gain a new perspective on your own life as you enjoy her musings about people, faith, friends, and life.

Jean Jordan *has written poems and rhymes most of her life. She was encouraged by her husband, Roger, to finally put her creativity in print. Both Jean and Roger pray you will enjoy the results as much as they have enjoyed the process.*

POETRY POD: Water with a Twist of Sublime

My Son

Jennifer Korell

Let me call to the angels for comfort
Let them put their wings on my heart
You see, my son is crying
I don't know where to start

Sometimes I don't understand
What to say or what to do
Please ease the pain you see in him
For what he's going through

You see, he's ten years old
He hasn't been here long
Help him Lord to understand
Help him to be strong

Make him kind and loving Lord
Show him that You're there
Teach him Your undying love
Guide his life through prayer

Guard him with Your hand
I know You'll do Your part
Keep him out of danger
I love him with all my heart

Christina M. Eder

You know how much I love him
Please listen to my plea
Wrap your arms around him
He means the world to me

So when it's time for me to go
I'll love you all the same
For you are my most treasured son
And Michael is your name.

My Son was written as a birthday present to encourage and comfort him. I wrote this after recalling a disturbing incident that happened to my son Michael when he was 10 years old.

POETRY POD: Water with a Twist of Sublime

I'm Praying for You

Jennifer Korell

Mommy and Daddy, I'm praying for you.
That God will bless and love all that you do.
I'm only a baby, so watch over me.
We have become a family of three.

Please God, protect my life
Free me from this strife
As I say my prayer to You tonight
I ask You share Your Holy Light

Protect me from all strangers
And those who do me wrong.
This is my prayer, Lord,
This is my servant song.

"*I'm Praying for You*" was inspired by a picture of my son folding his hands when he was a toddler. He is looking up with an expression I'd caption, "I'm praying for you, Mommy and Daddy!"

In fifth grade, our teacher, Mrs. Cannon, assigned the class a poetry scrapbook picture project. I received a good grade for that poetry project and wanted to write more.

My favorite story was *Cat in the Hat* by Dr. Seuss because I loved how it rhymed. In college, I wrote "The Teeny Tiny Town," a children's story with a rhyming verse. My tutor friend shared "The Teeny Tiny Town" with her students, who repeated the story during tutoring sessions. I submitted that story to *Highlights Magazine* and eventually began a book series titled, "Fishy Tales." The first book in that series is *A Day at the Beach with Shrimp and Friends* (available on Amazon).

Jennifer lives in Tennessee, where she writes music, illustrates and oil paints nature scenes and portraits.

POETRY POD: Water with a Twist of Sublime

Watching My Christy Grow

Carol Lynn Mahr

A babe in arms you were
It seems not long ago
I held you close beside me
As I watched my Christy grow

Soon came the walking
Then running to and fro
Hand in hand we went
As I watched my Christy grow

Then off to State Road (school)
You were all "Gung Ho"
So, arm in arm we went
As I watched my Christy grow

Next year was first grade
Pig tails and that new bow
You looked so sweet and cute
As I watched my Christy grow

On through the years
With recitals like a pro
I sat back and cried with pride
As I watched my Christy grow

Christina M. Eder

There were concert and games
And studies that would flow
Report cards never let me down
As I watched my Christy grow

Babysitting, working hard
Just to earn some dough
To help out with many things
As I watched my Christy grow

Soon to Aquinas High
With pride I see you go
All my love goes with you
As I watch my Christy grow

Good luck, honey
Give 'em Heck!

Carol Lynn (Celius) Mahr hand wrote her entire life from high-spirited motion. Every conversation, mission, craft and prayer became a poetic flow of her generous heart. When she moved to heaven in 2015, I found a handful of poems she wrote on her manual typewriter. "Welcome Home" and "Why I Like My Family" were typed on green copier paper. She penciled "Watching Christy Grow" on a scrap of loose-leaf paper.

I share these poems as gifts from her spirit. The world knew her as Carol Celius before she

POETRY POD: Water with a Twist of Sublime

took her married name, Carol Mahr. I know her as Mom. Mom, thank you for watching me grow!

I'll love you on both sides of heaven, Christy (a.k.a. Christina M. Eder).

Christina M. Eder

Why I Like My Family

Carol Lynn Mahr

It all began one summer
Two people much in love
Went to the wedding altar
A blessing from above.

Soon just one year later
A little bundle came
And left this twosome couple
No longer quite the same.

Now just a few years later
Two daughters and a son
To complete a happy household
In unity as one.

To do our duties can be fun
When it's done with love of heart
With good intentions from within
We finish what we start.

Each one of us is special
With no one quite the same
We learn this when we listen
To the others' dreams and fame.

It's not how much we have
Or what others find unheeded
Happiness is measured best
By feeling warm and needed.

POETRY POD: Water with a Twist of Sublime

Our home is like a stage
Each one must play his part
To make a house a happy home
Where blessings get their start.

Ups and downs are daily chores
To work them through in hand
Understanding is the answer
To make our home a better land.

To watch each child growing
With dollies, trucks and books
It's not how much we have that counts
But how our insides look.

We always tell the children
To love and laugh and smile
'Cause life's most gruesome trials
Only last for just awhile.

We go to church on Sundays
To worship, sing and pray
To praise the Lord for being great
And thank Him for each day.

Life would be so lonely
Without the growing love we share
Life would be so empty
Without family here to care.

Why I like my family?
It's simple as can be
They came from God in heaven
They mean the world to me!

Christina M. Eder

Coming Home: To Bob for Christmas

Carol Lynn Mahr

As I sit here and think
Of the days that have passed
I wonder if life
Is going too fast.

But recalling the months
That seemed too slow
I remember not twelve
But eight to go.

It was May he left
To a place called Cold Bay
Insignificant to most
To me, he's away.

Leaving behind
A daughter and wife
Who love him so much
A part of our life.

Being away
Is not to his choosing
But hard to accept
The time we're losing.

Yet his being away
Has meant more than just pain
Our future is coming
And happiness our gain.

POETRY POD: Water with a Twist of Sublime

Someone once said
And I recall it is he
That our love is much deeper
Than this separating sea.

To bridge those seas
Brings him so near
To La Crosse Central Airport
For Christmas this year.

The miles between us
Are many and far
But the love we display
In our family called Mahr

Eases the heartache
But not all the grief.
It's a blessing from God
To have faith and belief.

I remember the times
We sat and had talks
Of all things and nothings
While going for walks.

Through snow and rain
We never had a care
While enjoying God's nature
And all that we share.

I could write on for hours
And maybe sound smug
But we pride a good marriage
Understanding the tug.

Christina M. Eder

Although he's away
His strength I still seek
And remember the comfort
He'd give me so meek.

He's a man to be proud of
The attempts that he tries
Always seem to turn out
God made him so wise.

But even more than his wisdom
Much more than his look
He's the man that I married
In the vows we both took.

POETRY POD: Water with a Twist of Sublime

That New Girl

By Erika Mitchell-Diaz

You drive me crazy
You're frustrating, aggravating and needy
Annoying, confusing and unruly
I have to raise my voice and use that tone
It was quieter when I was alone
"Before you" is getting hazy
You're adorable, sweet and kind
Playful, and cross-eyed with a crazy strong mind
Everywhere I go you're soon at my side
Staring up at me with your ridiculously blue eyes
Ready to pounce on any damn thing
And carrying around that green mouse on a string
When you play with that mouse you cannot be beaten
Even though we both know you're cheating
All the different sounds, you have quite the vocal range
No idea what you're saying but that will eventually change
You drive me crazy
I can't wait for you to grow out of it
But I hope you never do

"That New Girl" was written about my cat, Ripley.

I rescued her from a shelter on January 17, 2020. When I got there, I found this tiny ball of white fluff curled up, sleeping in her cage. I knew she was a kitten; that was something I did *not* want; but she looked so vulnerable. I knew I had to meet her. As soon as I picked her up, it was decided.

I was on leave from work and wasn't due back for a few weeks, so I was able to be with her while she got used to her new digs. When I went back to work, it broke my heart to leave her every day.

The year 2020 was a hard one for a lot of reasons, but I got one amazing thing from it. I've been able to work from home and watch her grow every, single day. For that, I am thankful.

Erika Mitchell-Diaz lives in Southern California (with Ripley). Fourteen years ago, Erika lost the love of her life to cancer and has been trying to overcome that loss ever since. "That New Girl" is the first poem she's written, and she admits she did so under duress, because her mom asked her to ☺. She said, "Even as adults we still must do what our moms tell us. Thank you, Mom." Hopefully, if you are feeling sad, "That New Girl" has given you something to smile about, like it did for me.

POETRY POD: Water with a Twist of Sublime

Twilight Ballet

Rita M. Reali

The willow outside my window
    dances on the lawn
      stretching, touching its toes like a
        graceful ballerina.
It tap-tap-taps the glass with
    an impish finger
        to attract my attention;
  then waves
its wispy branches like a thousand
    slender arms, beckoning
        me out to pirouette with it
  in the clear April moonlight.

Many years ago, I worked as a one-on-one paraprofessional for an eighth-grade boy in a public magnet middle school in East Hartford, Connecticut. As part of the poetry segment in the language-arts curriculum, students were tasked to write poems in a variety of styles.
    This was a non-rhyming bit of poetry I'd toyed with while my grumbling charge was busy grousing about having to do that "lame" exercise.

Rita M. Reali is a onetime radio announcer, music director and news director who's been a sought-after editor and proofreader since the late 1990s. She's an award-winning novelist, whose Sheldon Family Saga has captured the hearts of readers since late 2015.

A 2013 escapee from Connecticut, Rita lives on the picturesque Cumberland Plateau in Tennessee with her husband, where she enjoys singing in her church choir, all things culinary, and writing a weekly blog at https://persnicketyproofreader.wordpress.com. Email her at rita@persnicketyproofreader.com.

Family Trees

Rita M. Reali
(writing as Gary J. Sheldon)

Grandpa was a mighty oak,
  his presence strong and sure.
And while we sometimes tested him,
  his patience long endured.

We swung from sturdy branches; and
  we played amid his leaves.
Although this must have tired him,
  he seldom seemed aggrieved.

He led his family skillfully,
  with kind and loving ways.
And when his gaze on them did rest,
  a smile lit his face.

My grandma, Jo, was strong and true,
  but graceful, too. And mild.
She was a fragrant lilac bush
  with the outlook of a child.

Her love for Grandpa kept her strong
  'mid seasons of trial and pain.
They stood together, two brave trees,
  through raging hurricanes.

Christina M. Eder

Since they were trees, my father was
   a Dutch Elm, tall and dark:
Both lean and strong; alas, diseased
   as well... and with a nasty bark.

I guess there's truth to what they say
   that fruits land near the tree.
From my elm tree of a father sprang
   a little nut like me.

"You're the apple of my eye,"
   'Gamma Jo' would always say.
And Grandpa would just smile at us
   in his knowing, special way.

He sheltered us and loved us well
   and gave all he could give.
When Grandma died, he summoned up
   the will, somehow, to live.

And live he did, for many years
   without his light and love...
on earth, at least; but knowing still
   she watched him from above.

Now a grandson of my own
   totters slowly 'cross the porch
to hug his Grandpa, tall and kind –
   a strong, yet yielding, birch.

Grandpa was a mighty oak,
 his presence strong and sure.
Though he's been gone now 20 years,
 his legacy endures.

Gary J. Sheldon is the fictional lead character in several novels in the Sheldon Family Saga, a seven-book series by Rita M. Reali. He penned this poem while reflecting on his past and how elements of his family tree have shaped multiple generations of the Sheldon family.

Gary is afternoon-drive DJ and music director at Z97-3, WZBX-FM, a fictional radio station in Middlebury, Connecticut. Married to Michaela (Conwaye) Sheldon since 1990, he's the proud, if weary, father of Erin Elizabeth, Amanda Josephine, Michael Joseph, twins Christopher James and Josephine Grace, and Edward Paul. Gary's a first-grade religion teacher and runs Mayhem Productions, which produces two weekly syndicated radio shows, "Rock This Way" and "Retro Rampage."

Christina M. Eder

Resurrection

Wesley D. Sims

The skirt of lush green grass
trimmed, he scrubs with vinegar
solution the dust and stains
from every letter carved in granite.
Washes and polishes her monument
as though it's her new house,
until it gleams in slant of evening sun
like the angel brooch she often wore.
Places a bouquet of robe-white roses,
kneels in front of the shiny marker,
back bent with crippling grief
heavy as a wooden beam.

Touches the emblazoned cross emblem.
Runs his fingers over the cuts
of epitaph as though reading Braille,
his eyes blurred by streaming tears.
He begs again her forgiveness
for the wrongs that strained
their relationship at times,
for salt sprinkled in open wounds.
And for his sins of omission—
the many times he denied a warm
embrace, an unrestrained kiss,
a heartfelt *I'm sorry*.

How often he missed looking
into pleading eyes, declaring
with heartfelt emotion, *I love you.*
Now he pours passion
into too-late words and misplaced works
as if a tidy gravesite and contrite heart
might call forth a resurrection.

"Resurrection" was published in *Songs of Eretz* in the Summer 2020 online journal.

Backstory on *Resurrection*
In 2019 my cousin and I published a book about the cemetery where many of our relatives are buried. We spent numerous hours in the cemetery reading stones, collecting records and stories. It was interesting and rewarding. For most of a year my mind was heavily immersed in those names and details. That led to writing several poems. After creating the book, I read something that triggered the image of a man mourning at the gravesite of his deceased wife. That seed started this "Resurrection" poem, and my imagination took over.

Christina M. Eder

Perspective

Wesley D. Sims

When I awake, look out this winter
morning, no brilliant orange fireball
ignites the Eastern horizon.
A cold, drab slab of gray smashes the sky.
My shoulders and chin droop
with accumulated grief and recent
disappointments—grandchildren
and other family members sick,
my own invalid weeks
constrained by a hospital bed.

Then I remember the story
of my great-great-grandfather
during the Civil War, surviving
three years in the woods
to stay near his wife and kids
and avoid conscription
into the Confederate Army.
How one frigid winter day
in 1865, the beginning
of a dark and sorrowful time,
he crawled inside the carcass
of a deer he'd just killed
to salvage its body heat
to coax his numb limbs
to push him on home.

I turn back to the comfort
of my safe, warm house,
walk to the deck
to replenish the bird feeder,
a down payment
on a Spring of birdsong,
and *will* my lips to begin
a song of Thanksgiving.

Backstory on *Perspective*
One gloomy winter day I felt discouraged by illness and recent events. I recalled a story of my great-great-grandfather during the Civil War. He lived in the woods for three years to be near home and avoid conscription. In 1865, late in the war, things were getting tough in the South. On his biweekly trip back home to get supplies and check on his family, he killed a deer. It was a blessing to have a fresh supply of meat, but it was so cold outside that once he got the deer field dressed, he crawled inside its carcass to warm up before traveling home. In reflecting on that story, I felt ashamed and ungrateful because I was blessed in many ways, especially with a warm home to live in with my family.

Christina M. Eder

One Unknown

Wesley D. Sims

No name or information posted.
Only an old brown field stone marks it.
We don't know if the person entombed here
in this small cemetery was male or female.
Other unmarked sites exist here,
so I will assign this one female.
Might have been a distant cousin or aunt.

Age and status unknown.
Parents and heritage unknown.
Was she old or young, a small child?
Death caused by smallpox, pneumonia, child-
birth?
Was she rocked by a heart-broken
parent or did she rock a child in her last
days?
She could have been a wife.
Maybe a beloved mother.
Did someone cry at her death?

Who shared her dreams and fears
that vanished in this patch of country soil?
Any descendants or relatives forgot her,
never came to place a tombstone
or any marker with name and dates.
Why was her grave abandoned

by everyone who knew her?
I planted a single rose by her stone,
retrieved from my grandmother's bouquet.

Not a nameless ghost.
Should not be another Jane Doe.
She was some mother's darling.
Possibly a father's pride and joy.
Born a member of the human race,
she had worth, deserved remembrance.
She was a child of our Creator
and He who knows when a sparrow falls
must have grieved her passing.

Backstory on *One Unknown*
In 2019 I worked on a book about the cemetery where many of my relatives are buried. I spent countless hours in that cemetery reading stones, collecting records and stories. Several graves of unknown persons feature unidentified stones or markers. The tragedy of deceased people in those unknown graves caused me to write this poem. I imagined who the person might be, what their relationships might be and whether they were mourned.

How I came to write poetry
My first exposure to poetry was Mother's Christmas *Ideals* books, which included poems and stories. She read them to me and, as

I grew older, they touched my heart enough to read them myself.

I studied poetry in English literature in high school and had to memorize excerpts. I didn't understand them or fall in love with them, but I didn't dislike or object to studying them. Some of those memorized snippets stuck with me. In church, the spiritual music moved me because it was essentially poetry set to music. As a late teen/early adult, a few poems in our local newspaper resonated.

My mother enjoyed writing notes and letters, but didn't have the education for creative writing. When she died, I felt like her writing torch was passed to me. I felt like this was a big nudge from God. Soon after her death, I took a poetry class at Pellissippi State Community College to gauge my writing talent. I enjoyed the class and discovered I had a gift for writing. I started attending writing conferences and seminars and, over time, I wrote and developed inspiration and an avocation.

Why I write poetry
I feel an inner urging to write, to communicate what I see and feel about God's awesome creation. I write about people I've known, especially my parents, grandparents and ancestors. I want my descendants to learn about my family's events and anecdotes as I knew them and remembered them. I want to leave my poetic creations as legacy and perhaps motivation for my children and grandchildren. I came to believe it is my destiny to write, a fulfilling response to an inspired calling.

Wesley D. Sims has published three poetry chapbooks: *When Night Comes* (Finishing Line Press, 2013); *Taste of Change* (Iris Press, 2019); and *A Pocketful of Little Poems* (Amazon, 2020).

His work has appeared in "Artemis Journal," "Connecticut Review," "G.W. Review," "Liquid Imagination," "Pine Mountain Sand and Gravel," "Novelty Magazine," "Poem," "Poetry Quarterly," "Bewildering Stories" and several others. He lives in Oak Ridge, Tennessee, and enjoys reading, writing, camping and gardening.

Amazon author page: amazon.com/author/wes4words
https://wesleysims884296882.wordpress.com/poetry-of-wesley-sims/

Christina M. Eder

Jonathan Livingston Seagull Bakes Sourdough

David Stratton

(*Jonathan Livingston Seagull is a story of a young seabird who, after being cast out by his stern flock, goes on an odyssey to discover how to break the limits of his own flying speed.*)

Having a fit alone being alone
a fit difficult and easy
at the moment fitting of panic
fits of what to wear if no one is looking
looking for and having a fit
For those unfit
With little here and less there out there
Jonathan Livingston Seagull bakes sourdough

Where we fit
Where we don't fit
Having fits
Where we are
Where we can't be

We fidget and squirm
Unless it was our idea
We choose to pry
to chance, pride, and privy

POETRY POD: Water with a Twist of Sublime

if we don't fit from a flaw
it seems apt
if we are held from an untested fit
it seems stolen

Sourdough starter needs a past without us
it came before us, to be without us, before—
the joy is then having a fit
making, joining, and a blossoming
like yeast and time

cooped up
held back
told what to do
weary what to wear
sourdough starters are shared

before we see a fit
it doesn't fit the picture
as a puzzle piece turned upside down
how puzzling most see
often forgotten
to forget
family
friends
a morning bird call
helping unstick a flat tire's lugnut

Fit often does have a fit.
doesn't want to be found

but to each piece gifted
where we don't—aren't
where we are
where we can't be
fitted

more there and where
having a fit
not noticing,
wearing a fit, where,
Jonathan Livingston Seagull bakes sourdough.

I wrote "Jonathan Livingston Seagull Bakes Sourdough" when I noticed we are capable of sharing while at the same time we're determined that our plans are executed as we dictate or the whole plan is smashed. It's as if we are perpetually both teenager and Merlin. This is not to say I am pessimistic, just the opposite.

    I see the *Jonathan Livingston Seagull* story as a model of finding a fit. Over the past year especially, I see we all have a fit somewhere over something. Fitting pieces together. We've been frustrated by being advised or told what to do. I've also experienced the generosity of my neighbors' not making too much fun of my Christmas lights' still being in my bushes in February. In the last year, putting puzzles together has become a growing activity.

POETRY POD: Water with a Twist of Sublime

Like a puzzle piece, sometimes it takes being turned around or lifted upside down before that fit is found.

Christina M. Eder

She's Gone

David Stratton

(From the Girl Scout song, "Eating Worms." Most versions have variations, such as the following lyrics I recall)

Bumps in the road
expected
are to be

*"No one likes me,
Everyone hates me
I guess I'll go eat worms,*

*Slimy ones,
Fat ones,
Skinny ones,*

*Slimy ones go down easy
Skinny ones wiggle while they go down
Fat ones get stuck in my throat
'cck, cck'
'cck, cck' "*

As our tears flow
With days to live
She talks of bumps in the road
And sunsets to admire and amazing

her grandson.
Choking on worms
As the song goes
Is a bump in the road
Expected yet
Presented and spoken

a calm I can't recognize
my awe
jealousies
fears
flow

See you later alligator
82 yrs. to 9
After while crocodile

Singing Girl Scout songs
Trivia ditties from the fifties
Recitations station to station
Recalling names dates and lyrics
In stride not missing a beat
while I forget what day it is with little fuss or
fare

This bump in the road
Affirming the road is here and not there
is not, well,
swell.

Christina M. Eder

swell,
seemingly seems apt for a pun,
a *swell* causing wings flutter or stall
a *swell* of needed updraft wind,
a swollen eddy,
a lack thereof,
as the room goes to tears
a choked up guffaw
from bruised breath.

In a sudden lack of—
swell.
seems seemingly apt.
Funny.
Sad.

Bumps in the road.
Yeah yeah.
Take the good and the bad.
 'Cck cck.'

See you later alligator
82 yrs. to 9
After while crocodile

"Slimy ones go down easy
Skinny ones wiggle while they go down
Fat ones get stuck in my throat
'cck, cck'
'cck, cck.' "

I wrote *She's Gone* about a dear friend who retired at 82. A month ago, she had new hip surgery and tested clear for colon cancer from three years ago. She was recently told she had three days to live because the doctors found substantial cancer outside the edge of her stomach. Limited remediation was possible. I visited her for three days and in five days she was gone. On the fifth evening, I received a text simply saying, "she's gone."

I am unofficially adopted into her family. During those five days she received family with her usual Girl Scout wit and calm stories. She had been an avid Girl Scout trainer and song-lyric machine. During one of our final visits, she challenged her 9-year-old grandson in saying, "There are bumps in the road as well as sunsets which will amaze you. Take both as part of the journey." The room broke into tears. We remember her for being pleasant and educational. We remember her for being kind.

David Stratton: Bantering, curiously chatting, inquiring, finding "just the right" adjectives. Fixes rusty bolts on an old car, brushes dog hair, and hikes in the woods to observe birds. He's a professor of art and graphic design at Brescia University, where he teaches studio drawing, painting, graphic design, and website software courses. He's been writing a book draft, *The Art of Mindful Lemming, The Process of Making Art*. For twenty-five years, David has been a freelance marketing consult-

Christina M. Eder

ant, graphic designer and studio landscape painter who has presented more than thirty solo exhibitions of his artwork.

POETRY POD: Water with a Twist of Sublime

Life at Bird Feeder

Sandra K. Stratton

> Early ones do get the worms
> Some loud-quiet-selfish
> Few share and feed mate
> Fat-slim-tall-short
> Being fearless-scared-wait
> Hurry-or-mean-gentle
> Bully-patient-old-young
> Happy to sing because they want to
> Picky ones-or buffet full
> Building a nest with sticks
> (Smarter than we are)

Life at Bird Feeder was written in 2021 when I paused to consider our 62-year marriage that has resembled ducks and birds. At 82 and 83 years old, we have a daily routine. It includes filling feeders and going after squirrels, sometimes to steal food. Each day is important, no matter what. We may live differently but we return to a normal for us. Sometimes there are delays. Blessings come from new friends, neighbors and giving to enjoy God's world.

How I began writing
My mother, Irene Leonard, gave our family the wonderful world of books and words. She was raised in an orphanage and lived in the library. She was a great reader and even after 80 years and ill health, she used the computer

Christina M. Eder

and taught quality time. Our son David has many treasured memories of "Granny" and has developed a love for arts and culture into his life.

POETRY POD: Water with a Twist of Sublime

Omnipotent

Larry Vittone

Even now, a prophet sings,
As an angel displays her wings.
The very skies, blaze with red
While they chant, "God is dead."

Is it true that God has died?
And that his prophet here has lied?
And that even now as he stands,
Reaching for the heavens with his hands,
Is he still living the greatest of lies,
As endless tears leap from his eyes?

You can hear the sadness in his breath,
When informed of the Lord's death.
With spirit dragging like his feet,
He shuffles down a dusty street.
He knows that God can never die,
But fears that He will pass men by.
This final prophet has tried and failed,
All his prophecies have been assailed.
He disappears into the veil of night.
The death of God would serve man right.

Larry wrote *Omnipotent* when he was in his early twenties, during the Vietnam War. He saw the wrongs and made his point through his poetry with all the wonderful arrogance and insight of youth.

POETRY POD: Water with a Twist of Sublime

Invisible

Larry Vittone

So close I drift, so close to stay,
Matters not the night, the day.
Always near, could almost touch,
The fairest skin that means so much.
Enough love to hold me bound to her side,
But can get no closer, how hard I've tried.
Not permitted to show my being,
She must know without her seeing.
I cannot speak, I cannot touch.
This one so close, I love so much.

I know her thoughts, can hear her talk,
and always by her side I walk.
Sometimes, it seems, she stares at me,
But from her eyes I know she cannot see.
Why can't I speak and let her know,
That I'm always here and shall never go.

Invisible sprang from a time when we were on vacation with my mom and brothers, at the little house my deceased dad had built. My stepfather was joining us in a week. This was Larry's first time there and he was inspired by the feeling in the house. Now, fifty-six years later, it feels like he wrote it for me.

Christina M. Eder

The backstory of Larry Vittone's writing, from Sue, his wife of 48 years

I share these poems on behalf of my husband, Larry Vittone. Many evenings I listened to him click away on my manual typewriter, crafting poetry that he read me when he finished a piece. He hypnotized me with his voice and fascinated me with his words. I could give him any subject and he would come back a half hour later with a poem. He planned to write more when he couldn't work in his shop anymore, but he didn't get to do that. We lost him to cancer in 2013. We were together for a short forty-eight years. He was my best friend, teacher, mentor and protector. Going through his poetry and stories was intense. Some of his poems were as familiar as if he just read them to me yesterday while others were just long distant memories.

POETRY POD: Water with a Twist of Sublime

Whispers in the Night

Suzanne Vittone

A word was heard, a whisper in the night,
And I sat alone until the morning light.
I wondered all through the day,
What that whisper meant to say.
A word was heard, just a whisper in the night,
and when I woke, I was compelled to write.
Those whispered words came tumbling out,
And wrote the poem it had talked about.

I dreamed this *Whispers in the Night* poem just before I woke up one night. As the poem says, I was compelled to write it. I am sure there were more verses, but I couldn't remember them in the morning.

Christina M. Eder

Where Is God?

Suzanne Vittone

God is in the quiet just before dawn,
He is there when you take time for a yawn.
God is there when you're driving alone,
And you can hear him best when you hang up your phone.

God is close when you try to do right,
And he is there when you decide not to fight.
You will know that God is quite near
When you don't succumb to the power of fear.

So just quiet your mind
And don't shed a tear.
Just whisper your prayer
And God will be here.

Dear God, are you there? We thank you for the gift of this life and the next life with you. Please help us be good assertive listeners. Help us be patient.

Where is God was inspired by my husband, Larry, who would hug an oak tree every day and when I asked him why he just hugged that one tree he said it needed hugs more than the others. I was thinking about that when I started this poem. That was in May of 2018. In the fall of 2019, as I was taking a class on becoming a Steven Minister, I could see where this poem was going and finished it.

Suzanne Vittone. I have had many passions in my life, from dancing to being a carpenter. In the last thirty years I have loved scuba diving, painting and wood carving. Now I enjoy writing family history and putting stories and craft ideas for kids and adults on my website, www.Bluecat.com.

Christina M. Eder

Section Three

Final Words

Painting is poetry that is seen rather than felt, and poetry is painting that is felt rather than seen.
— **Leonardo da Vinci**

Christina M. Eder

Endless Counting

Make life count
At what pace?
At what price?

Make life count.
How fast do I count?
Who counts?

Stopping.
Starting.
Which motion?

Listen. Learn. Teach.
To whom?
From whom?

Measured. Methods. Leveraged.
What are benchmarks?
Who calculates?

Make life count
Count for what?
An incongruent quest?

POETRY POD: Water with a Twist of Sublime

Please RSVP

A free will invitation
God's gift of freedom
Freedom to choose
        to create
        to develop
        to love
        to teach
        to share
        to believe
Free will

God's invitation to join Him
Joining in generosity
        in gentleness
        in encouragement
        in creativity
        in courage
        in honesty
        in reliability

Sometimes my free will
is expensive.
His priceless gift
spent on my costly choices
Free will to be good will
Please RSVP

Christina M. Eder

Speak Up

Father,
Was that a Yes?
Help me obey.

Father,
Was that a No?
Help me comply.

Father,
Am I to wait?
Help me be patient.

Father,
Is that my path or someone else's journey?
Help me walk straight.
Let it be so.

POETRY POD: Water with a Twist of Sublime

Dinner Time

Come
Follow Me
Join Me for dinner
We'll eat at My
table of Life
Catch some fish
Bake some bread
Bring wine
I'll provide
food for thought and
fruit of the Spirit
All are welcome
Invite friends
We'll multiply
our celebration
Eat heartily
Enjoy our
Last Supper together

Christina M. Eder

Deployed

Trials and tribulations
Assignments and alignments
Smiles and celebrations
Both sides of lessons and blessin's
An earthly internship
Learning heaven's business

POETRY POD: Water with a Twist of Sublime

Peace in Pieces

Piece by piece
    Grant me peace
Whole
    Still
Calm
    Gentle soul
Pieces
    at a time

Christina M. Eder

Perpetual Poverty

"You will always have the poor among you, and you can help them whenever you want to. But you will not always have me" (Mark 14:7).

    Poor decisions
        timing
        upbringing
        education
        relationships
        eyesight
        hearing
        nutrition
        neighborhood
        health
        motives
        priorities

    Rich in Character
        in Mercy
        in Grace
        in Truth
        in Compassion
        in Gentleness
        in Integrity
        in Abundance
        in Love

POETRY POD: Water with a Twist of Sublime

      in Peace
      in Wisdom
      in Understanding
      Provision for the Perpetually Poor
Vast   Infinite   Priceless

Christina M. Eder

Universal Obesity

Overweight
Heavy minds
Crowded hearts
Burdened spirit
Packed agenda
Bloated stomach
Personally stuffed

With what?
Food?
Overscheduling?
Fear?
Heartache?
Confusion?
Ego?
Entertainment?

Information
Without transformation
Invitation
Recalibrate scales
Everlasting measures
Wisely saturated
Flooded in forgiveness
Dripping with joy
Gratifying silence
Abundant space

POETRY POD: Water with a Twist of Sublime

Room to spiritually mature
Free spirit
Full filled

Christina M. Eder

HAIKU

Haiku Verse

Unity. Structure.
Five, Seven, Five. Counts grace in
Syllabic patterns.

Last Respects

Sun shifts its spotlight
To invite full moon to shine
Changing of the guard.

A Moon's Lullaby

Goodnight sunbeams. Warm
Another half of our world
I'll light earth's evening.

Summer Delight

Strawberry ice cream.
Vibrant pink creaminess melts
Down my sweaty arm.

Some More Summer Delight

Chocolate, marshmallow,
Graham crackers marry under
Night moon's campfire coals.

Circle of Life

Ring of fire. Ring
On a finger. Ring around
The rosey. Circle back.

Christina M. Eder

Surrender

Selfishness choking
Rooted pride. Release constraint,
Freely levitate.

One Smile at a Time

Murderer. Killer.
Warfare weapons. Kindness. Care.
Guilty as charged.

Cake Walk

Funeral. Birthday.
Wedding. Baby Shower. Cake.
Celebrating life.

Lucky Verde

Lime green frogs. Bug-eyed.
Child-like curiosity,
Living on the fly.

POETRY POD: Water with a Twist of Sublime

www.ingramcontent.com/pod-product-compliance
Lightning Source LLC
Chambersburg PA
CBHW071902070526
44583CB00016B/1806